To: _____

From: _____

10X QUOTES

# 10X QUOTES

by Grant Cardone

# MESSAGE FROM GRANT

It's a pleasure to present you with my *10X Quotes* book. The quotes and images included here are based on the principles I wrote in my best seller, *The 10X Rule, The Only Difference Between Success and Failure*. My goal in putting this book together is to provide you with an aesthetic reminder of what it takes to succeed in business and in life. Keep it on your desk, bedside or coffee table so you can refer to it often.

We all have dreams and goals that are worthy and we should all do whatever it takes to attain those goals. Too often our day-to-day routines, distractions, challenges and possibly, negative people can divert us from our targets. The *10X Quotes* book is your fuel, your motivation, perhaps that one little push you need to get back on your game.

I know you've seen quote books before but I trust you will find this to be 10 times (10X!) more valuable than any other you have owned. It's hard hitting, to the point, aggressive, even a bit in-your-face to wake you up at those times when you find yourself a bit off track. It's an excellent way to get the attention of those hard-to-reach prospects and makes a great gift of appreciation for your customers and employees.

I truly hope you enjoy these images and quotes; we loved putting this together for you. May the *10X Quotes* book leave you inspired, encouraged and with a renewed interest in taking your life to 10X levels. Tweet me a selfie holding this book @GrantCardone and I will hit you back.

Wishing you a 10X life,

Grant Cardone

Work like you are
getting paid 10X
your wildest dreams.

# 10X ATTITUDE

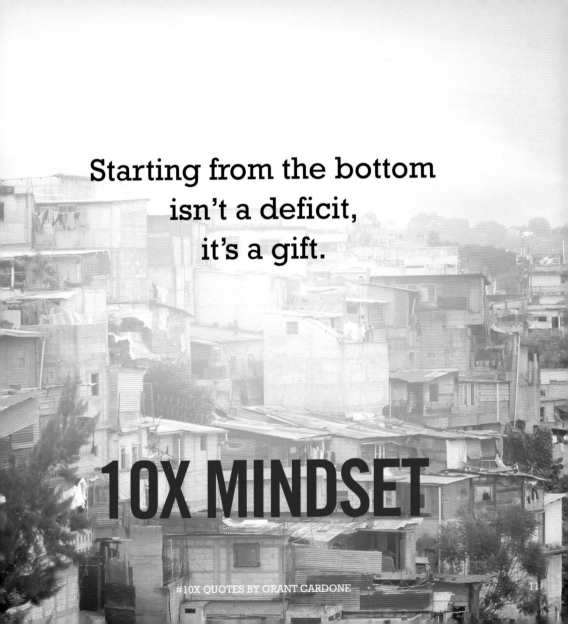

Starting from the bottom
isn't a deficit,
it's a gift.

# 10X MINDSET

The right level of action
is massive action.

# THE 10X RULE

Never seek balance,
seek extraordinary.

# 10X LIFE

Let the rest
do whatever
while you do
whatever it takes.

# 10X EVERYONE

Eat what you kill
is the new economy.

# 10X HUNTER

Set goals that match
your potential,
not your ability.

# 10X GOALS

Courage isn't the absence
of fear but an urgent
impulse to do something
despite fear.

# 10X COURAGE

No matter how it may seem,
no one has control
of your life but you.

# 10X CONTROL

Make time
not excuses.

# 10X PRIORITIES

How far you have come
is less important
than how far you can go.

# 10X FUTURE

There is no shortage
of money on this planet,
only a shortage of
people going for it.

# 10X MONEY

The only reason
for retreat is to
prepare an attack.

# 10X ADVANCE

Build a fire so big and so hot
that even your competitors
stare in amazement.

# 10X FIRE

Persistence is the single
most common trait
of the most successful.

# 10X PERSISTENCE

If patience is a virtue,
urgency is divine.

# 10X URGENCY

Normal is the most
dangerous level of action
you can take.

# 10X NORMAL

Success is my
duty, obligation
and responsibility.

# 10X SUCCESS PLEDGE

Real power
only comes from
repeating actions.

# 10X REPETITION

When you can't find
your "A" game
keep taking action—
it'll find you.

# 10X ACTION

Adding time to
a decision won't make you
more confident.

# 10X DECISIONS

The best seats in the house are never better than playing on the field.

# 10X PLAYER

If you are flying
under the radar,
you'll never
launch into orbit.

# 10X ROCKET

The person who suggests
your goals are unrealistic
has given up on his.

# 10X TRUTH

I am not interested
in fitting in.
I am interested in success.

# 10X SUCCESS

Money flows
to those who get
the most attention.

# 10X ATTENTION

The more I do
the more I realize
I can do.

# 10X LEVELS

Success lies in the gap between where you are and your potential.

# 10X POTENTIAL

You won't achieve
massive success
without attracting haters.

# 10X HATERS

Commit first,
figure the rest out later.

# 10X COMMIT

Thinking big takes
the same amount of effort
as thinking small.

# 10X THINK

I never trusted my talent,
so I outworked everyone.

# 10X YOUR TALENT

"I don't have time"
is the biggest lie
you tell yourself.

# 10X TIME

Keep showing up
long after your competitors
have given up.

# 10X GRIND

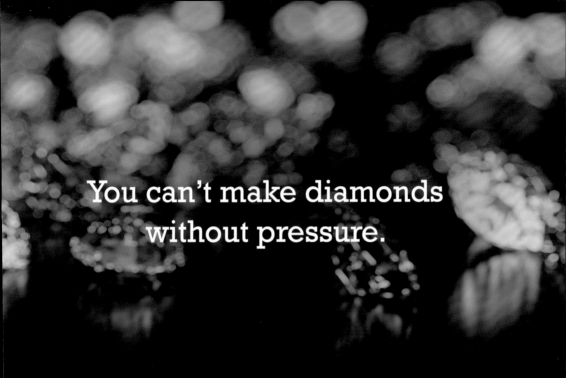

You can't make diamonds without pressure.

# 10X PRESSURE

If you're not first
you're last.

# 10X DOMINATE

Don't go to work to work.
Go to work to prosper.

# 10X PROSPER

One week they love me.
Next week they hate me.
Both weeks I get paid.

# 10X BOSS